# BELOVÈD
# BEAST

# BELOVÈD BEAST

*Poems by Dennis Finnell*

9.26.96

For Joan,

May you enjoy these.

Dennis Finnell

*The University of Georgia Press*

*Athens and London*

Published by the University of Georgia Press
Athens, Georgia 30602

Designed by Betty Palmer McDaniel
Set in Electra
by Tseng Information Systems, Inc.
Printed and bound by Thomson-Shore, Inc.
The paper in this book meets the guidelines for
permanence and durability of the Committee on
Production Guidelines for Book Longevity of the
Council on Library Resources.

Printed in the United States of America

99 98 97 96 95 P 5 4 3 2 1

Library of Congress Cataloging in Publication Data

Finnell, Dennis.
Belovèd beast : poems / by Dennis Finnell.
p. cm.
ISBN 0-8203-1708-X (pbk.: alk. paper)
I. Title.
PS3556.I4969B45 1995
811'.54—dc20 94-29149

British Library Cataloging in Publication Data available

*To Anita*

The buds will go on swelling,
The rush of green will explode,
But your spine has been shattered,
My splendid derelict, my age.
Cruel and feeble, you'll look back
With the smile of a half-wit:
An animal that could run once,
Staring at his own tracks.

—*Osip Mandelstam*

# ACKNOWLEDGMENTS

I thank the editors of the following publications, where some poems first appeared:

*American Literary Review*: "Dickinson Mound Rest Stop, Western Illinois," "Grotto," "On the Taconic Parkway at Nine Partners' Road"
*The Chariton Review*: "Fame and Fortune"
*Denver Quarterly*: "The Bed," "The Irish Wilderness," "Real Poetik"
*The Illinois Review*: "The Generic Manifesto," "Rapunzel, Rapunzel"
*Laurel Review*: "Ballade, U.S.A.," "Invasions of Privacies"
*The Massachusetts Review*: "Acmeist," "Letter to Wang Wei, Envoy to the Barbarian Pass"
*New Letters*: "Bonfire's Story," "Hannibal, Revisited"
*Passages North*: "Martyrdom"
*Pequod*: "Hanging Bridge," "Kiss"
*Prairie Schooner*: "Cupola"
*Santa Clara Review*: "Book of Days," "Our Epictetus," "Rapunzel, Again"
*Southern Poetry Review*: "The Book of Moonlight," "The Last Sky"

I thank the Ragdale Foundation for residencies during which a number of these poems were written.

My thanks also go to Mary Fister, Mary Koncel, and Margaret Szumowski for their patience and support.

And thanks once more to David Graham, co-respondent.

# CONTENTS



## VERTEBRAE

## REAL POETIK

# BELOVÈD
# BEAST

# HEADLESS HORSEMAN

I come from St. Louis. This may explain this tic I have
Of squinting, at any hour of the day or night,
As if asking, "Is that Katrina Van Tassel
Getting on the bus to Sleepy Hollow?"
Then again I am the namesake of the patron saint of Paris,
Who cradled his head like a baby in his hands down from Montmartre.
He carried it into his grave, resting in peace with it, at last.

St. Louisans put faith in their eyes—within reason
And a couple blocks—and we citizens,
To a child, don't trust the graph paper world of Descartes.
Thus, we have perfected the famous "rolling stop"
At intersections, looking both ways, then both ways again.

We do hand it to René, however, when it comes to doubt.
We could in his honor add under the fleur-de-lis
That graces our city's flag, *Cogito Cogito*.

It's not that we break down weeping and publicly
Confess every little pyramid scheme to some local newshound
In some Borgesian Garden of Forking Paths,
No. It's just that we've studied the history of *adieu*,
Which boils down to fifteenth-century out-of-the-body travel
Through the vehicle of perspective, from which we catch sight
Of the head of John the Baptist, belittled,
Horrified at his own martyrdom. It's on a platter for Herod's Feast.
Salome is nowhere to be seen, unless
That splotch with its back to us is her.

We've studied good-byes
In streets that radiate in a stilled

Explosion, that all along promise us a sun at
The center, a kind of geopolitical model of the Big Bang.

What's more, St. Louis doesn't end at eye level.
It goes on to an underworld of catacombs where good solid burghers
Took picks and dug out subterranean
Biergartens as their neighborhood grottoes. St. Louis summers
Went on stewing overhead, smudging the sunset, sentencing
The less fortunate up above to try sleeping in bathtubs.

It's just that each of us remembers a long, hot ride
In a rocking streetcar, growing seasick
Riding downtown, a thousand miles from saltwater,
And remembers resting a head (which kept saying *I'm going dark*)
On mama's lap, and keeping our fingers crossed that being
Grown up was not being seasick, except at sea.
Imagine our surprise, growing up.

Years pass. A man ends up in a stick house,
Surrounded by snow-capped mountains, which demand a lot of attention.
*It has come to this.* The mountains are his pupils,
And the first lesson is this: he resides on 27 Road,
Just twenty-one one-hundredths of a mile north of H Road.
*I don't know if I'm going to like*
*This teacher,* says Grand Mesa, looking down
Into the green grid of the valley, at a pictograph of a house.

This man writes down what he swears is the winning number,
And scrawls a map to Shangri-La, all in ball-point
On a niece's hand, which the man squeezes
Tightly, for safekeeping (and maybe just a little good luck?).
The little girl draws his portrait, and he
Kisses her on the forehead for it, puts it away in a book.

Years pass. Things fall out, such as hair.
Each winter keeps plowing more furrows in the brow.
A book opens, of course, a portrait falls out.
It is and is not his head, there on the Big Chief paper,
Which, itself, is a haircloth of slivers, and filaments from rags.

*Oh, you're not going to like this face,* I tell my old friend Brom Bones
From Sleepy Hollow. *Let me have a minute with it alone.*

Give a little girl a pen (which is tantamount to
Plucking a feather from Cupid's wing, then handing it back)
And she'll draw a picture of her uncle's potato face
Without a neck, none at all. The hair will be a ragged afterthought,
A ruse for the skull, against its awful confrontation with space.
A handful of whiskers dotted and dashed in on the chin, and full
Lips, slightly crooked in the embryonic stage of smugness.
Ragged mustache, attached to the nostrils by a thread.
And the eyes, behind what look like
Glasses held together at the bridge with black electrical tape,
My right eye in a perfect, effortless wink, without one wrinkle,
And the left one wide open, like that Egyptian hieroglyph for our hard *r* sound.

Years pass. I was born in St. Louis. Little did we know
How dark we would go, how even the grottoes
To the Virgin in blue, upended bathtubs, and the neighborhood watches
And cornboils, the new chains of burger joints and the feasts to John
Would do little but spray our souls with bad words in Day-Glo.
You didn't know about the piece of sky ahead of time,
Did you, the one your fiancé would bring down on your head,
Even though the city ordinance clearly called for everyone
To look both ways first. But you'd occasionally raise a little H
When a scheme for justice would fall out and crack and ooze
All over the soapbox. Some system. *Some egg.*
You would grow up with a big pie-face, as if

Long ago with The Bookcliffs peering over your shoulder
You drew your future self-portrait, drawing mine.
Maybe people do this all the time, ignoring
It, claiming it's a coincidence when at the intersection
They run into their biological moms. Don't tell me
What's become of the map on your palm, or the winning number.
Imagine their surprise. The song says we still got a long way to go.

# VERTEBRAE

# ON THE TACONIC PARKWAY AT NINE PARTNERS' ROAD

Straight ahead looms the ghost called the Catskills,
Aloof, homogenized to a blue-gray by distance
Where Rip is catching forty winks
In the petting zoo, as children touch his long beard
And jerk their hands back, worried it might come alive.

If a storm is itself and a soapbox oration
Belittling our life and love, if silver lightning
Scrawled its insignia on the slate of the Catskills this instant,
If that agent called Thunder then came, I would believe
Small, jovial men were at ninepins in the mountains once again,
But believe it only within the realm of my car.

You understand, your face is over my shoulder
And there are too many true stories about turning around
To see just once more—a face, a city in flames—
And someone gets turned to salt, to stone, or is exiled
In the underworld, after which someone else is torn limb from limb
Along the Mediterranean, these tales repeated for ages.

Most of the world goes on without us
And sometimes right through us, in x rays of our faces
Or as infrared images of illegals,
And only much later do we discover how they harm us.

Today's radio will tell of a marital disturbance
With a neighbor turning to discover
The cause of gunshots, and being damned herself
As the abode of the shades of the dead,
Seeing her friends that way.

As for me, it's a two-day soliloquy
Beyond mountains and great lakes, through Babylon
With its pork bellies and corn futures,
To a room where my back will be kept to you.

# DISTANT MEN, DISTANT TREES

Indiana has relieved Ohio on the afternoon shift
Of parading the straight legions of corn
Past the passenger window, past the forgotten eyes in my head,
Which is preoccupied with the busywork of distance.

Car stopped, the body's memory of morning travel
Is a noise in me, a crowd doing the Wave,
And somehow I believe that offering up the steam
Of this vegetable soup to my face will quiet that interior,
If there is one, still. Should I mention this
To Sherri or Carrie or Roy, the Mr. Donut people?

Naw. They'd only think, *Easterners*,
Then say, "Have some more soup, have a fresh donut."
Vegetables. Wheat. They aren't even grown out there,

I want to bet Roy, what with Mr. Donut
Being a big chain and the global economy and all,
But Roy has disappeared.

Here, what is believed?
That distant men have no eyes, distant trees
No branches? Or that a thing can be small,
Taking its integrity to the horizon, and beyond?
You could stand in the field, turning like a dervish
And pointing the beam from your finger out there

Saying, *End of the world, End of the world, End of the world . . .*
And still the distant woman stretching up
To hang sheets out to dry, would travel to us.

Once a woman and I lived in a Midwestern farmhouse,
All those rows of Goliath corn giving
Daily lessons on parallelism and perspective,
Diminished in our eyes by the David of distance,
How a stalk of corn meets its neighbor, but beyond the Midwest.

Our farmhouse grew dark as gingerbread
And the world sneaked inside, buzzing in summer after our blood,
Cold, whistling, arm-in-arm in winter. Remember?

Now she is on the other end, studying the Armada of clouds
From another screened porch, as she waits out Johnny the mailman,
Whose face has sixty-plus winters
Written in it, and whose stooped shoulders bring
A note recounting the saga of cornsilk, enclosed.

# GROTTO

Just through the winding circuit of three-storied mansions,
Just playing deaf to the echoes hailing us
From the walled estates, reminding us of who we really are,
Just being a little more patient and we shall see
The lake, a seam of darker blue through the trees.

Then it's simply the stairs zigzagging
Down the bluff face and we're there, where the lake
Breathes in a way, more sedate than the Atlantic
But out there the horizon is nevertheless water against sky.

A man sits on a wrought-iron bench, shirttails
Out and a two-day growth on his face.
Each bench features a brass plaque with a donor's name
Etched in a gothic manner
And we who sit here see things partly in their names.

The man is not myself, we are very different men.
He watches a woman I will call Venus
Sunning herself alone, oiled, turning more happily brown
And as she rolls on her back as in bed
She is unable to hide a flaw, and he feels closer.

Late summer bees are lingering, exploring
Openings with odors, and some colors—
The wooden trash bins and a soda can,
My mouth, and I notice the flyaway hair of Venus.

Each of us needs a small, empty place
Lined with sea shells
Where his next breath comes from.

The cooling towers of the Zion Power Plant
Stand the beach just north, and I think of castles
Of the future, all in rubble—like Dunstanburgh in Scotland
Apparently dead before it could reach the North Sea.

When Venus notices his looking
He turns to the white cursors of the sailboats
(One of which I know is called *Miss America*)
And soon looks again at her darkening body.

The tops of a few Chicago skyscrapers
Peer over the lake's horizon miles and miles away,
Rising, flooded, no one will say.

# CUPOLA

Most of the world here is as invisible now
As your small, raspberry beauty mark
So what's left but the day's cupboard of images
And tomorrow's promised deliveries, the rumble
Of a commuter train speeding along the lake shore,
The ambient voice of the lake forever asking, *Kiss?*

The stairs squeak, it is dark.
It's like climbing up into a community head,
And more—being able to peer out
As though from gems bejeweling a head
And seeing things, even backwards
So that finally we have eyes in the back of our head.

There should be pigeons here, there should be feathers
And guano on a hay-strewn floor,
But this is also home for the Night idea
That up here a person is the squared and plumb locus
For whatever needs to rise,
This cupola, abbreviated steeple for lay believers.

Are there walls around you? Is there speech?
In darkness, are all distances the same?
Is at least part of you emptying itself
Into the night, like a pitcher being poured on the moon,
And the dark side of the moon at that?

Maybe it's just me, but up here
It's a real job with few perks to surmise
That everyone down below is asleep,
That the sleep of most will be rich and blemished.

It's a job to pass their nocturnal work along,
Another sandbag for the bleeding wall
Standing against the Zuider Zee.

So please grant one a bird in the hand
That is simply a bird in the hand,
Grant another swimming privileges
And another sex like it used to be
And still another that a son not fall in the jungle gym
And still others for an apartment without insects,
For an eternal struggle, for the hair of Rapunzel,
For the next buoyant word, for a tree or a picture of a tree,
For a stairway down tonight,
You on the landing, my eyes in your hands.

# KISS

Most of us believe Lake Michigan will win
Its long, nearly breathless seduction of Chicago.

In a new oral tradition Cupid will be all abuzz,
Whispering inside the ear of Adler Planetarium,
"Let the lake have you," and Eros
Will walk Shedd Aquarium to the long bed of sand.

Then stars will lie down with fish
In a peaceable kingdom inside the lake—

But that's eternity we're talking, not this morning
As the Lake Shore Limited hustled us along
Between the lake on the left, the city on the right
With its high rises looking
Quarried, hewn into something human, dragged
Shoreward and propped there, brooding lakeward.

Even the Art Institute was a talisman
Meant to ward off the lake, but giving shelter as well
To four hundred photographs telling the story
Of fixing shadows, and people paid their respects,
Shuffling the maze of walls of pictures, and nodding.

In your favorite one a couple is kissing.
The city goes past them in a blurred pantleg
And in unseeing faces under a beret,
Behind eyeglasses, under a postwar hairdo,
In a trenchcoated man with hands held behind him
As he makes his constitutional, in the curved
Rim of the sidewalk table whose job is to gleam.

In the background City Hall is a ghost of itself,
Unfocused, peering over their heads
So parentally there should be a story about it talking,
Saying, *Ah, to be young again, to have a real face,*
Remembering itself when it was water and stone.

They are kissing, and her hand is entranced, hanging—
Not exactly lifeless at her side, but as though
Life had been summoned urgently elsewhere.
They are kissing, and his hand is forming an O
With thumb, forefinger. They are kissing,
And their mouths are the still, quick, molten center.

In our long kiss, which one of us is city,
Which one of us is lake?

# BONFIRE'S STORY

To you lucky stiffs on final approach to O'Hare,
This big, black O on the Shaw prairie must be
Another way in and out, the opening
The dwarfs use to the mine inside Mother.

Yes, it's the '90s. Seeing me
Last night, though, you'd think *I* was mesmerized,
Walking in a dead march toward the flames.

Fire seduces, then leaves us with ashes
That stare us down forever, and do not burn.

Last night bonfire's story was the one about
Summer's emaciated limbs being turned
To gold, burning on the prairie in a giant mound.

Now a black O is smoldering, a vowel
For you still airborne, talking your way down . . .

But fire articulated another
Last night in the flames split like crows' tongues—
Once a woman was one walking, talking
Desire, and if you opened her up then and there
You'd have seen it was an empty
Niche, opening in a stone wall, readied for a likeness.

Some of her was reduced to a blue urn's
Contents, and rationed by her husband to the sea.

Now her spread ashes are permanent guests
Inside leviathan, whose watery song

Questions the sea for the other, without rest.
Lucky ones, has your descent been long?
Soon enough is O'Hare, whose strips of concrete
Are a character where two stories meet,
One of fuel, one of oxygen.

*—In memory of Crystal MacLean*

# THE GENERIC MANIFESTO

Today, Sunday, September 10, 199____,
Ensconced in the form-fitting chairs of the Burger King
That spies across at the Edens Mall, now deserted
Because of a Blue Law (which is a forced,
Silent march to the hymn "If It's Good Enough for God, . . .")

And lonesome as American Sundays are lonesome,
Where the six-day-wonder-of-a-world
We love, finger, and put on our gold cards is exiled
To the Monastery of Memory, or to Monday's Theme Park,

We hereby declare "The Generic Manifesto"—
Not that there's anyone else here, just my Whopper and me.

Everything looks like something else,
And today it's that other thing that concerns and awes us.

New, unruined buildings hunker down along the strip
Like a gauntlet of ungilded bunkers—
A layer of concrete or a metallic fascia imitating cement,
Then a layer of tinted glass that intimidates
Us, reflecting our own failure at seeing,

Flatters us with our darker, brother images,
Gives us the willies, as if each
Internal compass were jammed, quivering like a water witch,
And we are up to here in Anywhere, U.S.A.,
But not that town guarded by righteous row crops
Where Bowser, knowing citizens by footfall,
Lifted his toy mongrel head to bark at a select few.

Now here is so interchangeable with there
That homonyms are endangered, that this is a kind of paradise
(Or is it "pair of dice"?) where a pit bull
Is barking, attacking something pitiable.

We're just becoming godlike, provided
God is vague, everywhere—like the plasma
Brooding inside and over our major cities, speaking of which,
Go ahead, stand our cities on their heads (as someone
Close to me has concluded of women) and they all
Look the same. A ______ is a ______.

So please don't alarm self at disorientation
As you peer into the other's horizontal face on the pillow.
It is always the morning after the night before,

And that queasy stomach and wide-eyed
Ignorance at where you are, and what you did, and with whom—
Hell's bells, we all feel that way.
It's the Hall of Versailles Syndrome, all
Those mirrors generating subjects from one king.

We, the undersigned, therefore believe
Meat and potatoes are our bread and butter
And as we bring home the bacon
We shall be drawn down the strip and past
Structures and green vegetation and one firmament,
Drawn by a formerly horizontal face pictured
Standing vertical in the doorway, beautiful—
But then again, whose face shall not be?

# RAPUNZEL, RAPUNZEL

You could feel your way to Lake Michigan.
You could play blind, touching each estate's wall
As you step through Lake Forest to the bluff,
The designer beach below, and water
Kept so comfortable, in civilized waves,
That drowning would be joining the best club.

It's not that villagers here carry clubs,
Or see better than you, to Michigan.
They're just protecting the sheen in the waves
In the hair of their daughters, behind walls,
Hair pouring over the girls' shoulders like water
Preserved in strands, draped over a bluff.

Don't misread their blank surfaces. It's no bluff,
Those clean, wordless walls to a rumored club
So private its code name sounds like water.
Feel along the walls toward Lake Michigan
And you may end up in it, period, end of wall—
Unless dumb luck in the shape of a wave

Spits you back on the beach. Then you could wave
Off the big lifeguard and stare at the bluff
Where like a golden ladder down a wall
A girl's long, blonde hair descends. You'd feel clubbed,
Spit up like that by Lake Michigan,
And then hair like spun gold let down to water.

Then Life would have some choice: crawl in water
To Wisconsin and beach yourself as a wave,
Or climb from the beach at Lake Michigan,

Hauling your hefty self up the private bluff
Using a girl's long, blonde hair. At the club
The smart money says you'll climb it, like a wall,

Since you can't swim. You're up against a wall.
What's worse? Lake Michigan's cruel water
Below you beating driftwood into clubs,
Or the scissors to which the hair with the waves
Leads you? You could trace the hair from the bluff
To the crime scene facing Lake Michigan—

Your name scratched in a wall, a Scotch and water
And a golf club with your prints, and the bluff
Lit up by a golden wave breaking in Lake Michigan.

## HANGING BRIDGE

Now the insects carry their work into the night
And since I cannot remember dreams,
Except the great ones or when startled from sleep by a noise,
I count on their music when I wake.

Once long ago the voice of the Mississippi
After the Missouri paid its tribute of soil and jetsam and water
Was a half-heard, half-conjured moaning,
A sound like a neighbor unjustly ill,
Which it may have been, partly. But what persisted
All summer in St. Louis were locusts,
And I woke to them and came back, morning after morning.

Music is more than a biography
Ghost-written, uttered by hand puppets.
This morning's crickets and catydids were still using
Their own bodies to sing their lives of love and fear,
And as I walked they ushered me along
To stand under the arching limbs of an elm, remembering—

The sky did not fall on us
After the chain saws took the sick trees apart.

The legs of the Eads Bridge grew from stones
Out of the Mississippi, and we as their little masters
Were passed along like secrets, never drowning—

And so this morning I also returned from memories,
Following a small, penciled map
That guided me toward The Hanging Bridge
Whose name yesterday fell from the lips of a friend.

*Let them call this a river,* I thought,
Standing, a little queasy, on the hanging bridge.
A *kid could swing over this using a good rope,*

And then I told my own fortune, looking
Into the clear-watered ditch of the Skokie River.

# INVASIONS OF PRIVACIES

Soon the local dove will stop its five note song.
Its throat will cool, and its wings will ease to its sides.
Soon a shadow will part from its host in the hour
Between the bird and the moth.

Hours like these give us pet names for use in the dark.
*Honey. Peaches.* And someone holds a finger and a thumb
To her lips and whistles, *Time to come home.*
Hours such as these drop

Gauze over the neigborhood. Now it might be wrong
To see the fat boy in blue running shorts
Kicking the little blue spruce, or wrong to smell barbecued ribs
Between the Finches' and the Millers'.

A drive in the car does no good. The light mothers all.
In the back seat of a cab a face from the Neanderthal
Is lit as Alexander's. Light graces every hitchhiker.
Isn't that B, an old buddy?

Isn't that gray kitten by the road an old pet called Midnight?
This light only publishes the past.
Even a lawn's plastic deer tells how dusk is a mule
Bred from the night and the day.

Staying home is ignorant. A june bug pounds at the door,
Needing a witness. It will just roll over on its back.
Ugly wind chimes and horselaughs and shouts for Billy
Make themselves right at home.

So in this hour break and enter the crossbred light.
After all, dusk hangs the private
Lives of neighbors in the air as if they're out to dry.
Step into dusk. Take them down.

This is the egg of what will be. See how the gauze posts A
At her window, her hands clenched at her throat?
Covet her. Wonder if she gestures from need or from fear.
Midnight and noon, come home.

# HANNIBAL, REVISITED

What if I told you the Mississippi is a joke of a river now,
That the silver bridge that would hum a mile-wide
Note with us and with the Impala's bald tires, it's now all oxidized,
That Huck and Nigger Jim work the inclined streets,
Mouthing their rap for chump change, and carving toy rafts,
That no one was auctioned here, that *Hannibal* is a nonsense word?

Could you then spot the new me as I walk head-on
Into a fence that is whitewashed daily, and see the enlarged
Eyes of Hannibalians watching me bump into their solid, blank world?
Their eyes ask point-blank, "Where are you from?"
I may as well say, "The other side of the moon."

Order a man to just try eking out a life here
Some years ago in four dirt-cheap, connected rooms,
Let the rooms articulate with one another like a four-word
Imperative sentence: *Live; sleep; work; eat.*
And you have the makings of a house of bricks,
And against it a man scratching his back, waiting for the bus
To talk him across the Mississippi, to look back at a rusting bridge.

But give that same man a piece of luck
That he bends over to pick up because it flashes on the sidewalk,
Do that, and someone like you steps out of a cloud and breathes
And revises our rooms from command to declaration: *We live and*
  *sleep and . . .*

And so today there are as many Hannibals as there are eyes,
Most, but not all, tricks with smoke, with mirrors,
Buildings, shoulders dreamed up out of something burning, something
  flashing,
That turn out pretty real when you walk into them.

Today black people walk in our rooms on 6th Street
Where once, out of sadness, I pinned your wrists down with my knees.
Do they walk through the ghosts of us in our old rooms,
Sleep on us, eat sitting on our laps?
And don't we ache from them, this nostalgia, this home-pain?

The man in the window scowls down at me, across the street,
And I should answer, somehow, but my heart is a jar of smoke.
Instead I turn on my heel and begin limping off
In a kind of three-legged race
Into the present, toward a silence that is a mile wide and brown.

Say something so I know where you are.

# FERTILE CRESCENT

Though I played with cards in the crib, my first cradle of civilization
Was a green polygon and two meandering blue lines.
There was a map pulled down like a shade, and on it a nun outlined
With her rubber-tipped pointer the khaki-colored sands, soon to be nations.

Even at recess I repeated, "Tigris and Euphrates, . . ."
And for extra credit pinched clay into Hammurabi's wise face,
And memorized Ur, Abraham's birthplace,
All for gold stars, Sister Siena Marie's.

Then naptime, when my life's labors truly began.
I could not disobey, looking again
As Lot's wife had,

and so I closed my heavy eyes,
Lulled by the swish of Sister's long black gown,
My head on my desk, watching even now
Children harvesting poppies with their fathers' long scythes.

## THE BLOODY BROOK BAR

Most of us were sober and saw our hands
As non-fists on the bar, and caught mirrored
Glimpses of an older woman, liquored
Up, waiting to sleep with one of us lambs.

That bar named for a local massacre
Attracted few tourists, save for those who wet
Their whistles on Bloody Marys and forgot
The mass grave, until some wiseacre
Said, You seen one hillock, you seen 'em all.

That night the bar's big-screen TV was a wall
Of a thousand gentle lights eating
Baghdad. We drank Bloody Marys to our fly-boys.

All G. recalls is someone who for
Fun sat on his chest until he couldn't breathe.

# THE BOOK OF MOONLIGHT

Last night a version of my mother's face
Flew in a sky at the end of a string.
It was moonish, with thick makeup, smiling,
And it was pulled down and it said, "Embrace

Me. Hug me." (Last time I held her she was
Already ashes, and I almost broke
Her, she was a dull vowel, like a schwa spo—
Ken as it shuffles a hall.) But because

Last night in this dream I had shaving cream
On my face, I could not hug her lean
Moonface. She smiled and said, "Be careful, dear."

The dead sit up all night. They keep an ear open
For our keys in the locks, but in their
Peepholes are the bloated faces of our messengers.

# THE LAST SKY

In the fragmented shade of a palm tree, eternity
Comes face to face with a long-limbed boy.
He lies there, spreadeagle on the cooled dirt, and he enjoys
A little telescope at his eye,

Its puzzle of wild, blue yonder. Stretched out like this he can gauge
How the weight of his own body is a big hand at his back,
Encouraging him, saying, *Take the sky in. Look—*
*Silver wings, and a face with a beard in braids.*

Now, forever begins. He has two brown eyes
That once saw ripe peaches, and now hold a winged beast.
His torso is a counterweight to the earth.

What he first sees as his beautiful angel begins
To tremble, in the fronds of the palm tree, in his cheeks.
It's blue and brown, and it breathes as one thing.

# MARTYRDOM

That night no sheep in a fold on the Amherst Common,
But people exhaling a gray *Amen*.

They mourned in a circle, with single, hothouse
Roses in canning jars, and an inner
Circle of short, nervous candles and incense,
Circles insinuating a small universe.

Some of us hawked the news of the burned man.
A slow child remembered his white finger
Pointing at hard words, a neighbor remembered
One night his *Peace* screamed down on the Common,
An old professor thought of Billy Budd.

Some protestors drove by and leaned on their horns
As mourners gazed at their constellation.

He believed one thing and swallowed its tongue.

## POCKET FULL OF POSIE

Sometimes the world is nothing but one face
And a finger, pointing. It says, "You there,
The tenth one. Show us your neck. Give us your car."

Then our subject materializes
Finally, with a torn blouse and bared breast,
And we track Mademoiselle Liberty's scent,
For where eyes and nose lead, the head soon follows.

No more mobocracy, no more llamas,
No more city, head misruled by a gang of ideas,
No more long-necked, fleece-bearing, hidden animals of the self!

Just a big bonfire of martyrs & tyrants
Hand-in-hand round one mouth.
And the next world is pictures
Of you, still in one piece. Now you're God.

# BALLADE, U.S.A.

*—after one of Villon's "poems in slang"*

In a city who is my mother a John Doe turns less white
He hangs from a metal tree    He shows how gravity works    How the
  world turns
He's been pruned    He's been grafted
By angels who sweet-talk pain    They make it flower
The wind muscles in from the Mississippi    It frisks and loots him
But he's blooming up there    He's the black rose
Put your hand in your shirt    Make a fist    You know what to do
Neighbors have thumbs    They have forefingers disappeared—
"Now count to ten    Now covet somebody's purse"—
Beaten in our name    Beaten in the name of strength

Say it's real dark    Say you're looking for Someone Small    Someone Rich
Rent a child's eye at the corner to spot angels
Don't wear white    Don't use your name    Don't even smell
Somebody might say    "Meet this lady    Meet Ms. Uzzi"
And you'd lie down for her    You'd be your own effigy incarnate
Say it's real dark    Say you're jogging in Forest Park
Remember Big Questions    But don't forget the Bigger Questioners
Angels who can alter you    We're talking forever
Your outstretched arms    They won't match
Beaten in our name    Beaten in the name of strength

They'll cuff you behind your back    Guard each curse with your teeth
You'll curl up in your mother of a room    Don't even think
Of yourself as clothes    Think of your body as dirt    As in "burial park"
An angel might hang you out to dry
And time is going to be going very fast in your back

Bent over    Worn down by the glacier
Don't dream    Don't give your fears or your loves that right
You might do two things at once—Sleep and speak in the ears of angels
You might pay them a tongue    Yours    Mine    Your lover's    A stranger's
Beaten in our name    Beaten in the name of strength

Sir    Words escape between teeth
When angels look the other way    Take a nap    Sometimes just blink
And spit gleaming on a chin    Sweat glistening on a forehead
  They're prayers
Against a tree    Against a knock on a door    For a glass of milk
Beaten in our name    Beaten in the name of strength

# THE BED

There are beds, and there are beds,
And this one scaled for a long-legged child
Is just right to rest the eyes, tired of believing
What the insistent light claims for the day.

Back there the lit world
Is a paradise for skeptics, with enough
Walking wounded to be touched,
Enough holes in the wall to enter, to taste.

Long ago I was a poor excuse
For desire, or even for a snowman
Standing in a park, awaiting fate near the seesaws—
That is, until you paraded by, answering
A late winter spaciousness with legs,
Reason enough for the coal in my face to see.

That walking manifesto said the beautiful
Never winters in the South, but lives year-round
Inside the gray, clapboarded Englehardt Apartments,
Kept behind a skirt and stockings.

There's the universe, it seems, and Kirksville,
There's eternity and an April day,
There's a farmer seeing your legs again, walking
The horizon, as he plows to the mock orange windbreak,
There's an old woman mouthing something
At your back, remembering his beard against her ankle,
There are girls who would borrow your legs
For the night, just to slay a few local boys,
And there is myself then, off in Never Park
Running one finger along a silken, imagined thigh.

The daylight makes its claims
To reason, and then the night comes along,
Like now, blowing a big hole in that argument.
There's a button with a picture of legs
Resting on the windowsill, and beyond that
More of the night, and beyond that, legs: yours.

## DICKINSON MOUND REST STOP, WESTERN ILLINOIS

Everywhere you look is the glacier's answer—
These ghettos of corn, a bed of soil called loess
So like talc between a thumb and forefinger that it spells
The end of dirt, the beginnings of faith, or its lack thereof.

Everything in this perspective goes so uniformly away
From an imaginary point right between my eyes
That I am my own dot and circumference,
Which makes me an angel, true, but an angel who is as lonely
As the red barn in the distance must be, keeping time, echoing.

All morning I have run over the yellow kernels spilled on the blacktop,
A number of them as the tires roll over them
Sounding off with a *Ping . . . Ping* . . . not a final plea but a parting insult.
Since I know many things, believe the kernels
Make up a trail of spent sunlight, between fields
Of harvest-trampled stalks and the wooden banks called corncribs.

What can we hold against the winter?
What body can we offer him for his pleasure?
How can we bribe him, how can we blackmail him, how can we
  convert him?
What weapon can we hold against his temple of snow?

All around me radiates the best argument for invention: flat fields
Growing fuzzy in hedgerows at the edge of the world.
People have seen fit, then, to lay the dead ones down,
Curled up on their sides, clutching clay figurines that become

More them as they become less themselves,
And to keep piling on the powdery dirt that has blown from the world's end
Until this "desert," this "prairie," stops the wolf in the cold wind
With a mound, and a dead one sucking at the teat of dirt.

If I'm so smart, tell everybody who the farmer is
In his parked truck who leers at me
From his face of tooled leather as I step
From behind the spreading oak tree, zipping up my fly.

## SPLIT INFINITIVES

To leave this distant land & a girl called Honey. To no longer
Root in the slop, but to rise back up on hind legs,
Staggering, squealing, out of the pigpen. To snap down
A gold card (my bonafide signature prostrate,
Face down on the counter), going nearly the limit on it on a rented
Air-conditioned Ford Escort, with CD player & dual air bags.
To wave a cloven hoof goodbye
To my pals in the sty, shouting *Bonne chance,*
*Brother pigs!* To turn my razorback on them, thinking,
*Heck—I was just a lottery to them, & now*
*The legacy's evaporated. It's turned into a cloud,*
*& a teeny one at that, shaped like a birthmark.* To

Set out, the sun at my back, the shadow of the Ford Escort attenuated to
Airy nothingness, my snout growing longer,
Almost human, & then to have that big herd of clouds
Running all over me from New York & Pennsylvania & the great
  beyond on invisible legs,
My head itself a small cumulus cloud on a string now,
With committee work going on inside, a real down-
Er, like five birds inside a bramble *thinking*—
But not singing—five different songs. To see my own monster shadow
  prostrate
Itself to a Scranton hillside of murdered cars, their last chance
For reincarnation at the world's biggest junkyard (where Life is clear:
  it's rented,
Just like the air inside the Ford Escort's air bags).
To enter Ohio, my shadow a long freak behind me now, howling
  *Goodbye . . .*

To drive into planet Earth's umbra, that same *Goodbye*
Dogging me past Indiana & Illinois row crops. To howl for my ears only, perchance to
Snort, all inside my rented Ford Escort. To interrogate my air bags:
*In whose image were you made? What's your raison d'être? & what's longer,*
*Life or my proboscis, your air or the word?* To weep near Terre Haute, feeling rented,
Mr. America's "date" for this nonstop twenty-three-hour odyssey. To rather be a cloud
(Our most beautiful animal, vegetable, & mineral of chance,
Even with stilettos of lightning, without one bone of compunction, without these legs,
These spines, making us walk upright, unprostratable
To any Mr. America), but—and this is a big *but*—for now
To spy the future's gold dot in the Ford Escort's rearview mirror, & to be thinking,
*Tomorrow's sun at my back! ahead the cloudbank held over down-*

*Town St. Louis—a guillotine of cloud on its eventual way down.*
To hold my breath. To asphyxiate *Goodbye*
As the Chain of Rocks Bridge chants me across the Mississippi, that un-thin king
Of waters. To be suspended, my own guillotine of breathlessness. To
Be in the crosshairs of time, *now,*
On this stone bridge back across, over this Mississippi, the bags
Of my lungs squeezed empty, until the Chain of Rocks Bridge goes prostrate
On the other, the Missouri side. To think, *Long, longer,*
*Longest,* as I suck in my "native" air, as I get my St. Louis breathing "legs"
Back, from the pawnshop of clouds over the sign of the Arch, rented
By other lungs since I left this burg, rented by chance
Oxidation, the bridge incarnate red, rented by clouds.

To return to St. Louis as prodigal as a cloud.
To feel like shit, driving the air-conditioned Ford Escort down
Market Street, past windows I dressed one summer with happy
  mannequins, on the off-chance
An Amy or a Bill might see me, & hand me my papers, soul, & throat.
  To instead get a big goodbye
In a blank oval face at 8th & Market. To drive these stations of my own
  rented
Cross of returning, past Union Station—where I parked big cars with
  tailfins—thinking,
*Now it's an urban mall; I'm an urban mall.* To pass the Fox Theater,
  where I first touched a girl's leg,
(& forever since just the phrase *The Sound of Music* brings to
My fingertips the biography of thighs), the Fox Theater no longer
A home for movies, but a museum of touch now.
To make a left turn. To recognize the "three"-bedroom brick ranch
  prostrate
At #1 Vale Court. To stop. To turn the Escort's engine off. To wait for
  the explosion of air bags.

To tilt the rearview & to see the decades bloated in the bags
Under my eyes. To open the Escort's door to August's clouds
& to have August's body all over me, nearly prostrating
Me, as if heat has missed me. To go down
On all fours in my heart, now,
With dad waiting behind the storm door, where chance
Meets free will in a belittled body, a face drawn down by the Earth longer,
As though lengthened on a cross. To whisper *Goodbye*
On his deaf side. To say sweet nothings to
His elongated face. To practice these truths that by the hour are rented,
& by the hour to watch his shaking leg.
To listen to his lips smacking, & as he nods off in the La-Z-Boy to be
  thinking:

*A child always thinks:*
*"The future's in the bag.*
*I'll have legs.*
*My mind won't be a cloud.*
*Pain won't rent*
*My lips." & the future prostrates*
*Itself Atlantic to Mississippi River to*
*Pacific day by day down*
*A filament of light attenuated to The Goodbye*
*Of Airy Nothingness. It's always now*
*The future shows us its back. It's no longer*
*Now.* & then, as dad sleeps it off in the La-Z-Boy, to buy a chance

From some black kid at the front door. To chance
Winning a big Oscar Meyer sugar-cured ham, & suddenly to re-think
The old life with Honey, how this ham could be me, but to no longer
Need the flesh Crusade, for a body is just a bag
For feelings, & thus to give the kid a crisp new one-dollar bill now,
Trading a certain randomness for a possible pig's leg,
A *real* fat chance, & thus to say *Goodbye*
To the kid & mean it. To turn back to dad's face-cloud,
His lips the dark lining thru which his old words come down:
*It was meet that we should make merry, & be glad: for this thy rented*
*Brother was dead, & is alive again; & was lost to*
*The pig pen, & is found, no longer prostrate.*

To then ride around St. Louis, as dad lies prostrating
The party line in his La-Z-Boy. To drive crazy in a school zone on the
off-chance
Some citizen might make a citizen's arrest, might take my face back to
Our mutual past, identify it, name me, & say, *Hmmm, I think*
*I know that guy. He's wonderful. I've missed him so much. I've felt rented*
*All these years without him. I'm no longer*

*Nothing. I've seen him again. Now life has meaning! I'll live forever. I won't feel down*
*Anymore.* To almost hit some kid on a bike. To have the Ford Escort's air bags
Turn the tables, interrogating me: *What do you think you are? A cloud?*
*You don't exist here. Take a number. You live on paper now.*
*Your city looks thru you, your father looks thru you. Say Goodbye.*
*You're paved over. Try standing up. Prove you've got two legs!*

To wake my father. To start his leg
Shaking. To cut four peonie stalks with unopened heads, the pink coronations prostrate
Inside them, one for each in the family—open they'll be a quartet: sing *Goodbye.*
To hear him ask, *Are those flowers in a jar? What's the chance*
*I could get a sandwich around here? Where you taking us now?*
To say back, *To Calvary Cemetery, to*
*Visit Mom.* To drive my father my cloud
Slow down the wide empty boulevard of St. Charles Rock Road, thinking:
*A parade for the victorious son. All roads lead from St. Louis. Everything's in the bag.*
To drive thru the crumbling legs of Calvary Cemetery's arch, past a rented
Green awning over a hole and a mound. To wonder how long the white goose down
Will float on the cemetery pond, *How much longer?*

To recognize some black kid wading shirtless in the cemetery pond. To wonder no longer,
*What is he doing?* Canada geese & mallards giving bay in a floating semicircle, the legs
Of his new jeans not rolled up, the kid bent over, looking down
Into the pond, his hands cut off by the pond, feeling for coins in the shit on the bottom, prostrating

The ferryman Charon below in laughter (he whose own skiff is rented).
To see dad mouth thru the car window: *Goodbye.*
To remember his story about his '38 Dodge, *before air bags,*
The radiator steaming, dad taking a chance
On the pond's water, dipping his fedora into it, running to the car, later
  thinking,
*I like this place. It saved me. I'll buy now.*
To see their plot, under the too-near big sweetgum with its crown a
  green cloud,
No upright headstone, but a brass-like plaque on the ground, *to*

*Make mowing the grass easier.* To walk behind him as he sidles up to
Her. To worry the sweetgum's roots are growing longer.
To see their pair of names in one flat brass plaque, which is the
  earthbound life of two clouds.
To look at his too-big pantlegs. To wonder whether he still has legs.
To see enough already. To turn my eyes down now.
To count: *three dates; four parentheses—two split infinitives.* To
  look down
Thinking, *They stole the brass vase, they ripped it from its chain,* thinking,
*I wanted a soul & she suckled me. Now that white transmigration is
  prostrate,*
*Nipples & milk, lips & soul.* To take a big chance
Anyway, letting the mason jar of unopened peonies weigh her down &
  so to head for the rented
Air-conditioned Ford Escort, with CD player & dual air bags.
To put my arm on him: a walking space, a dash, & a closed
  parenthesis. To say *Goodbye*

To his good ear. To feel his *Goodbye* leave its warm scrawl on my
  cheek, & to
Take my signed face & grab my travel bags, as prodigal no longer
As fire or water—more like dirt. To climb in the rented Ford Escort.
  To float a thought-cloud

Over St. Louis, one saying, *You too may have hind legs*
*One day. You too may lie prostrate in the pig pen*. To recross the Mississippi, now,
On the Chain of Rocks Bridge, arched like someone's back. To think, *Don't look down*.

# ACMEIST

The steppe is prose. It refuses to turn back
On itself, the way a child's rolling hoop will, or Venus or Mars.
It turns back on itself the way a wolf does, or a nation.
The grasses come up past a train's wheels and whisper the new facts of life,
*No use genuflecting here. You can't eat us.*
From the boxcar Acmeist Mandelstam sends his eyes on a courier's
mission,
Twenty, fifty, a billion *versts* to Siberia's end—a bungled horizon,
A smudged draft of the first imperative sentence.

Between the slats his two eyes, his nicotine-yellowed fingers
holding on,
Are punctuation: *Quote, period, period, unquote.*
Two eyes that report a yellow oval, blue-black wings, there! in the
bones of a birch.
His third eye identifies it: *Goldfinch.*
His fourth eye is cocksure—it's Anton Chekhov inside his rented
*tarantass,*
A goldfinch in a cage jolting along on unsprung wheels going to
question Siberia.
The Acmeist puts a hand out through the squinting slats,
Turns it palm up, offering millet seeds to goldfinch Chekhov.

He recollects Chekhov's words: "*Before Lake Baikal it's all prose.*"
And for the Acmeist, Lake Baikal is the liquidation
Of the steppe, its back turned on its earthen history at the smudged
horizon,
It is the ice-cold saga of empire, with a sky of goldfinches flying
In and out of cages on buoys, singing the glories of the Kremlin
mountaineer!

Lake Baikal was Wednesday, will be Friday, is never Thursday.
A bird has its wings clipped in mid-flight, in mid-song, and is falling
All day Thursday through the verses of Lake Baikal.

In Vladivostok he catches up with his eyes.
They interrogate *him,* from fish soup, from puddles, from the dregs
Of birch bark in his tin cup, and the agent who stands in his ear
   commands,
*Don't eat what's in your wooden bowl, it's Lake Baikal. It's poison.*
So the Acmeist makes believe he is the labor camp's scarecrow, eating
   garbage.
He turns to look back at his nation, nipping at his heels.
His eyes—two periods between which his lines have been excised.
His future reader is in his mouth, *like* a goldfinch.

# FAME AND FORTUNE

A famous man and his now-famous dog
Once slept fitfully here all night, under trees
Whose limbs now bear no fruit, but curve downward
From the heft of generations of apples.

The local wit says, "These trees are just big
Rosebushes, and the famous man is wind
Out of our mouths. He is just his words pinned
To a warm body—like boutonnieres, nametags . . ."

I point, count: Twenty-seven trees are stooping
In the orchard, still arranged in a quincunx.
Five rot where they fell—like dancers told to
Do so, or stars decomposing in old flags.

The famous man cuts an apple in half.
He smells it, his youth picking fruit and bites
Into it and squints: *some life we had, heh?*
The dog says, "Ftt, ftt," meaning *Feed me, master.*

But wait! The man is straddling a limb,
Carving stick people, arm-in-arm, in the tree trunk.
Shouldn't he be under a tree, sleeping fitfully?
And the famous dog is howling at the famous man.

# CORNUCOPIA

We felt the whirlwind, and never knew it
Had had a bad childhood.

                                        Once apples and wheat,
Asters and black-eyed Susans lived in a cornucopia.
She was a whirlwind, loafing on her side, bulging with plenty.
She had a teenage body then, of woven grass and asters
And a silly grin stretching from Atlantic to Pacific,
Our comic latitudes. In those years time would stop for no reason,
Daydreaming, leaning on a fencepost, then would go back to haying,
Or back to putting spokes in bicycle wheels,
And we ourselves, you and I, you without one name to your name,
Would fingerprint one another, throwing the book at each other.
No one got hurt, we were just local yokels, and cornucopia smiled on us.
But fate had a piece of rope down its pantleg.
Someone real tall told her everything was *ok*,

                                                            *just put your lips on it*,
And before you knew it we were eating our own dust, becalmed
In the tragic longitudes. Cornucopia stood up in all of her height and
   howling
Whirled herself and the north side of town away. Bulletins
Were issued, but things were never as they were, and in the stew of
   Spring
She descends as a larger-than-life comma, our *vento dei venti*, wailing
*This was Kansas, is now, and ever shall be.*

# OUR EPICTETUS

We depend on things that if put on cassette
Or videotape, or even written out in plain English,
And then played back later at home
With enough quiet, and maybe a cool drink,
Would seem insubstantial to build our lives on.

If you wrote down "air" or "foot,"
Or took a snapshot of your eating utensils,
Then wrapped it up like a present, later opening it
Alone in your bedroom, you might be spooked
At how your life is so . . . well, very, very menial,
And you might call somebody, even anonymously.

The ambient noise is our friend.
When it ruptures and the sirens materialize,
Or the whispers materialize for spare coins or shoes,
I, for one, feel let down by our friend,
Who is a wall of noise, albeit a wall of silk noise,
Letting the barbarians rip through.

It's like this: mouths have been grafted
On army blankets, on cardboard
Domiciles about the size of children's playhouses
That are squatters on the sidewalks,
From which pleas are hurled at us, as if
Anyone's life is snippets
Of pain, hawked on the street corner.

This is why I wonder about Epictetus,
For whom an empire was a vast diamond of an argument
For sensation, where pleasure and pain

Were whipped into making their daily rounds,
Where his master twisted his leg, passing time.

Didn't he arrive at his own blue law,
Following a road of sorrow, no son of a god himself,
To where the world led and ended at the Forum?

Now all these mouths are uttering his
*I told you it would break.*

# RAPUNZEL, AGAIN

What I recall is a boil of voices at my back,
And a big, deliberate step down under the tavern's electric lantern
(That looked a little like a pumpkin with a candle in it)
And a plan in my head to walk back to my room
With my eyes closed, feeling my way along the walled estates.

My shoes echoed off the walls. The night air was rich
With the odors of mown lawns, and something curried lingering.
Behind the walls there must have been roses named for daughters.

The night itself was a velvet curtain
That she parted and walked through, bringing her face.
It teetered, I remember, floating in the night, like a lotus or a buoy.

She began saying something, looking into
My chest, as though behind my shirt was my real face, and asking
The powers there to show her how to "cut off her neck,"
To help her lie down across the commuter tracks.

She carried a pillow under her arm, a ring of keys in her hand.
*No, you don't want to do that,* I said once I really heard.

Her hair was platinum, and short and spiked.
To all my questions she said *no*, or asked for my help,
All the while looking into my shirt pocket or buttons or pen.

*Do you have friends? Can I call someone? What's your name?*
*Do you live nearby? Can I walk you home?*

My eyes wavered between her face and the pillow under her arm.
*Please help me cut off my neck, I don't know how.*

I showed her my back, walked home along the walls, exonerated.

# LETTER TO WANG WEI, ENVOY TO THE BARBARIAN PASS

Our plans for the assault are final: we'll wait.
The mountain's not going anywhere.
And the chrysanthemum wine will only grow courageous.
Until then we rehearse, hiking the stairs in the blackouts.

The ninth day of the ninth month will come, speaking at last.
We will ascend Mount Tom, bearing the dwarf dogwoods
On our shoulders, like nieces and nephews to see the world.
We believe you are air and ashes.

Happy Valley will float in our wine—
Topsy-turvy, it's true, but delicious going down.
And the faces of loved ones in wine. . . . Enough said.
What remains are some characters on a scroll.

It turns out we're angels, not you.
A space where things travel—
The square where a voice is summoned,
The boulevard of spiced dumplings and a man whistling—
Between yourself and those who have just been joined to you.

Some domestic fowl are dead, some gone to the barbarians.
Each bears the flower that opened in the stone wall.
Let us know what you need us to tell them.

# THE IRISH WILDERNESS

Tonight I sit up with Ursa Major, telling him the story
Of the cultured pearl of our loneliness.

The eighteen-wheelers in this rest stop idle like dozing animals,
The kind that sleep, eyes wide, standing up in the pasture,
And each trucker, coiled up asleep in his cab,
Is the genii of his truck, dead tired.

The sky wants my head, of course,
In its maw, between a pair of twinkling canines.

Who, after all, understands desire's tongue
Of sibilants and fricatives, much less speaks it, if not
The one standing in her distant grotto of common sea shells,
Feeding a sparrow in her outstretched palm?

The one whose skin I love chafing against mine, whose soul
Is the blue-headed flame of a pilot light,
Has looked at me, more than once, the way a small cloud will,
And said, "Explain that one more time."

Long ago one Father Hogan on his mule into these Ozarks
Led a clan of Irish families, homesteaders
Pulling on their handcarts the Old World's carcasses
Of children and seed potatoes into the New World.

Now locals call it the Irish Wilderness, that plateau
Of limestone and scrub oak and freshwater springs mumbling insanely,
And today in broad daylight I hiked into it,
The chert gravel under my boots, coerced to speak,
Reciting its few choice consonants, and I repeat them for you two,
Great Bear who will eat me, woman with her tongue in my mouth:

One morning they disappeared, just like that,
Like a bowl of water in August, a plate of millet for sparrows,
They disappeared without trace, without logic,
The sustenance of the wilderness, an enactment of faith,

And today in broad daylight I hiked into it,
As I rounded a stand of scrub oak and their knotted gargoyles,
And I nearly disturbed the flock of vultures
Forming a black rose around a dead thing,

And you who house your tongue in my mouth
Don't see the beautiful wound.

# BOOK OF DAYS

There is no calendar here with a red covered bridge
Vaulting an airbrushed stream, and vaulting
Its double lying upside down on the mirroring stream,
No covered bridge looking like a village shrine
For all who dare a crossing, and looking
Like a beast peering down at its former, less
Substantial incarnation, or perhaps its future.

No calendar here, only a circular window
Beyond which The Unblossoming Elm Branch
Undulates on a breeze, acting
As umbrella over the bronze seal pup in the echoing courtyard
Who is made forever to spout water as a fountain
As he lies on his back, water arching from mouth to belly
That, in time, will be rubbed to a lustrous nothingness.

Under this circular window and unblossoming branch
There is no name or date, no holiday
Or advertisement for Burniske Heating Oil,
Only an underworld of hairline cracks in the wall
Under a round window, and smudged fingerprints
That add up the days and the disembodying distance
As well as any number or name, any contract on time.

Each day promenades arm in arm
With its own beatifying obliteration
Down the lane overarched by tree limbs to a point,
Simply to a point, vanishing, lustrous,
And in that romance of day and nothingness
We find our book of days open with facing pages
Torn out, each hoarding the other's.

I am a giant, reside in back of one eye,
So at the end of your dog-eared day,
As your trees, your fog exchange places for the night,
That diurnal tit-for-tat, that becoming,
You offer your profile to the window,
Refusing to let the light out, and letting
Yourself be taken by a stranger, a seer, alone.

So many attractions in this mean distance
Waylay us with their eyes, and want us
To ease in as part of them, a kind of home remedy,
But out there between a blur of taillights
And the worrybeads of knuckles, you are almost prepared now
To flick the switch, heading into your black office,
Nightgown on, the tumbler of water at your bedside.

The last thing is making the red X across the spent day
Under the covered bridge and saying, *Another day,*
*Another slash,* to the old gray cat whose eyes are orchids
Until a Saturday can be left blank, empty
As promises, promises, until memory fits desire
Again along a common, ragged border on a white Saturday
As the book is reassembled, time rebeginning.

By then I will have climbed out of this eye,
Done my deeds, seen my sights, and been readied to lift
The page to a canyon powdered with snow and holding space
That is our home.

# TONGUE. THE END OF THE WORLD IS ROADLESS. *EXILE*

The Danube has a mouth. Out of it the tongues
Of Europe pour in a polyglot stream,
And the Friendly Sea is the continent's black thesaurus.
Near the mouth I live in a noun,
*Exile*, with stick walls for consonants,
My own mouth open round as a vowel.
I have a name, and in Rome my old friends excuse
Themselves, bringing it up in public.
A new coin says in Latin and with the Emperor's
Face, it's year xxxvii of Augustus.
To get to the end of the world I could not march
On a stone road radiating from Rome,
Worn smooth by the Legions. To get to this town
Called Tomis (named after a man
Butchered here by his wife) I paced Rome's un-
Forgettable streets weeks on the ship's deck,
On legs I ended up naming *taedium* and *terror*.
I kept my back to home, to avoid my wife's
Face on the sea's wake. I offered her my back.
And from the wooden Nereid of a bowsprit
I looked into the three Seas and vomited
To their accompaniment, even into
The *pax* of the Bosporus and the friendly Black Sea,
Even my ration of Rome's hard bread
Exiled. The end is one large mouth and a score
Of smaller ones, none speaking the mother
Tongue. The end of the world is roadless. *Exile*
Means I hold my face and walk around
Inside the stockade, displaying it like
A baby held up at eye level—

*Look, my face is wailing, it is innocent.*
Nevertheless, the minutes parade by
Like Legions, and the natives treat me like a dog
They know, seeing it gnaw itself,
And let be. *Exile* means the red-haired
Girl I have put lips on me and breathe
As I sit on the riverbank, I call *Erato,*
After the muse. *Inspire me now,*
*Beauty, betrayer.* It means my ears thirst
For Latin, that the native tongue is dice
And the clack of dice, that with my own tongue
Nowhere, every unheard word of Latin
Is an ideal world—a stillborn Atlantis.
Out here, I am Rome.
I wear the skins of animals just like
A native and run helter-skelter inside
The stockade, dodging the barbarians' poisoned arrows—
*Taedium, terror, taedium, terror . . .*
What I do with my stick walls and open
Mouth is write epistles in verse,
*Tristia*, and send each year a book
Of these "Sorrows" to Rome. What I do is
What the red-haired girl does, posing
As letters of the alphabet. Her mouth
Opens for O. Legs spread for V. I grow erect for *I . . .*
Most air is liberated as it expires
At my mouth, and it walks off, sometimes limping.
It will walk up to the sky and say
Nothing. The air going into *Tristia* for Rome
Wears a long white toga. It lies
Face down at the feet of the First Citizen Augustus.
This air says everything. It says,
*I was wrong. Forgive me my dirty*
*Book about love. Please at least ship*
*Me where our tongue is spoken, where*

*An ear exists for my mouth. My real*
*Crime was to imagine love. My real sentence*
*Is to imagine Rome here by the*
*Danube's mouth. Out here, I am Rome.*
My alphabet turns its head, gazing
Back at me, a vowel in a bearskin. Inside some
Sticks I push a bowl of ink
Nearer a candle. The stockade is an O around
Me, an O on a page of the steppe.
My friend in Rome wears my likeness in gold
On his finger, my friend holds it to his ear—
*Believe Pythagoras. The soul follows the body,*
*Haunts its place of rest. I am*
*The steppe and the river delta, I am the Friendly Sea.*
*The months melted away like sherbets.*

## MISTERIOSO

That solo I'll take without rehearsal
Will sentence me to straight life without parole,
When the drums' *tempus fugit* commands, "Stand up. Blow."
And I'll kiss my horn in lieu of a certain gal,
And I'll blow, and blowing blow my life away,

While decades ago you will all but close
Your nightclub-reddened eyes, the better to hear me,
Or this coming Sunday you'll play the record, and peer
Outside at a neutral thing, like the river,
The better to see me, and all of us come home again

In the long, improvised osculation of music,
As insubstantial as breath, as freakishly beautiful
As inseparable twins at the sideshow,
And the evidence is not the still-tender cicatrix
That is my lips, but is your ringing ears.

# REAL

# POETIK

# REAL POETIK

Once I helped decipher a writer's posthumous papers. Before that
He had been a perfect stranger to me, except as I
Had caught sight of his putting one word in front of the other in *Knock on Any Door,*
His novel of, by, "The Proletariat." That's mean to say,
I know, a kind of lie, because his book was Chicago with a bay window
In it, and something very much like a man sitting in that window at a loss for words,
Whose mouth opened wide against the El, whereupon I
Screamed. His posthumous papers were the usual dead writer stuff—drafts
Of flawed masterpieces, the imperfections red-lined
And the new, improved revisions careted in, also in red, all
Looking like an illustrated bestiary, and versions
Of versions of stories, mostly of his own ambitiously herded life
As he walked his body up Mount Rainier, down Chicago's tenement
Alleys, rife with raw, metallic echoes and razor-sharp knowledge—
*I've walked all this way to fear.* "Posthumous papers"—sounds like the bills
And letters and junk mail breeding in the mailbox after death,
Doesn't it? Or the *Times* and the *Shopper's Bulletin* stacking up in front of the door,
Or his passport with his last photo coming too late, all
Because no one had been told the belovèd had died. Anyway, I'm squeezed
Into this TWA wide-body and I'm
Here to tell you the belovèd is dead. Long live the belovèd.
I think I'm flying. I may still be over California. I'm not alone.
My ears hurt, and there are hundreds of us facing east here,
As if for a sunrise service, when the belovèd will greet us at the airport.
I think we're heading to the center of the country where all the Belts
Meet—Rust, Corn, Bible, Goiter, in one vast cummerbund.
In derelict factories in Gary and East St. Louis the new corn cults meet.
Do they ever stop to think one moment about
The belovèd, jailed long ago and far away in East Thermopolis,
Wyoming. He put down his bedroll too near the town's belovèd hot spring.
It was winter. He was one cold colored man, a cinder in the snowman's eye.

There were no coins to jingle in his pocket, and his life and bad fortune were illegal.
He got thirty days. The cult members can find it all in his
Posthumous papers. It's all on toilet paper from the jail, in a neat script
As tiny, condensed as a colony of ants. These days
A man might write just any old thing down on an airline's paper drink napkins,
Because he's bushed. Let's see, it's 3:08 A.M. inside a wide-body.
The air coming out of the little overhead nozzles is telling us all
To take a nap, be good, shut up. *Pssst. Pssst.*
But Seattle's lights must be burning down below, out our port windows,
In a sky as dark, as stimulating as coffee, and someone like me
Must say, *Seattle's lights are burning. They were a kind of ark into which*
*Our eyes went, two by two.* And so it was that last night
A wide-body climbed up through Seattle's dark, low ceiling,
I *think.* (What's memory but negotiations between
Management and yesterday over who did what to whom—
And when—or settlement talks between this moment hissing from the air nozzles
At 3:09 A.M. and its spouse over childhood's custody.) I left Seattle.
There was no sky. It was exiled for winter. No problem. In lieu of a winter
Sky were artificial lights on buildings and islands, on rusting fishing boats
And undulating on black Puget Sound, duplicating the fake sky.
I left Seattle, left a heroine inside the city's self-made night sky.
She changed into her freedom suit treading water, holding her breath in the middle
Of a river, stepped barefoot on the riverbank, writing her name in mud. She said
That at the end of the line one must turn, or write homilies.
That fear at the end of the line is the gardener, cultivating the next breath.
That without a real sky we tell our own fortunes in the city's lights,
In earthbound constellations, the blue tongue of a lit match here,
A flashlight beam there casting a stranger into his own bust,
Headlights turning the corner home, the sidewalk, then the front door
Lit up, an island ferry in scratchings of light, the ferry's lights
Gossiping on the surface of Puget Sound, a few lights that must mean
Something big on Bainbridge Island, the rhomboid of a curtained window flickering
From TV light, the pinholes in skyscrapers, a Mickey Mouse
Nightlight. I left Seattle. From the wide-body it was burning. A city is
Its own sky anymore, with a fortune to be told at eye level,

With mortar and lit filaments. It's 3:11 A.M. inside
A wide-body. The air comes out of the nozzles overhead in homilies.
*Silence is good, naps are good. Patience is heroic. Think of the fir trees*
*Of Seattle, their convention of stoics.* But we who barnstorm for beeswax
Earn our red eyes, must spit it out that last week
Was Seattle, Minneapolis the week before, Detroit before that, and that
Next week is St. Louis, that a month is four cities, then *home.*
That's our calendar, with no picture of some Mount Rainier in alpenglow
As he was last night below us, out our port window.
He was smiling, his head of snow presented on a platter of clouds. He smirked,
He saw the white lies down the Pacific coast waiting for us at L.A.,
And not just its ganglia of lit cars, to and fro in exurbia
Under the air's gauze, not just the palm tree at the airport at its forced
Labor, standing in a big pot, orienting us, saying, *Welcome*
*To Los Angeles. Look, I'm a palm tree, see? Where you guys from?*
Not just the vending machine in the airport that would dish out espresso.
What's a mountain for if not to see for us? Mount Rainier smirked
Because he saw the blue tongue of the TWA agent tying
The truth in knots—*Your flight will be delayed briefly to St. Louis.*
Mount Rainier was glowing, seeing the airport lounge closed, the TV
Turned off, no heroic Letterman to save us, no
Espresso left in the machine. California closed, the belovèd nowhere.
We proles slept sitting up, we proles on the floor, prole
Heads on baggage, on another's prole shoulder, just a colony of bigger-
Than-life ants. What's a mountain for if not to see for us proles?
It's 3:13 A.M. aboard a wide-body. T-
WA has given us drinks, free movies. A man might
Write any old thing on a paper napkin. The big woman at my elbow
Watches without earphones Bogart as Nick knocking on doors, to redden
Her eyes. He's going to fry, but I won't spoil her surprise.
All of us aliens here face east, posted in orbit at forty thousand
Feet, hurrying our pairs of red eyes into morning, goosing the speed
Of sound, beyond which even a declaration like *I love*
*You* is percussive, a Saturday night special saying *Die bas-*
*Tard.* So in the syntax of powered flight, we are imperative: fly. But if

Lift fails, if the verb of the engine dies, or the subject (you understood) has
A heart attack, we are incoherent, a sentence fragment, mouths open
Falling all over the U.S. of A. Underneath the port wing
Eight miles of liberty, then the constellation of some city.
It looks like a burning strand of the national DNA, it looks like a homily
On fire. At my elbow she cries big tears as Nick is belted
Into the chair. All the gossip on the El is he'll break down
Like a baby. Get to know any light and it grows eyes, opposed fingers and thumbs,
It breaks out of the bestiary. We aliens know a few stars
By name—one calls herself Madeline—and we are as kites to them,
Tethered to down there, the string and the message we are passed along
Friend to friend, star to star, across the U.S. of A.
The big woman is done crying and leans her heavy head against the port
Window. The world out there is just beginning to show up again,
A little pink giving the clouds bodies. *Mount Rushmore,*
She thinks, *or just some cloud thing with four or five heads, maybe more . . .*
Nick is dead, long live the belovèd, long live the beast.

Dennis Finnell's first book of poems, *Red Cottage*, published in 1991, won the Juniper Prize from the University of Massachusetts Press. He has taught at the University of Tennessee, Mount Holyoke College, and Wilkes University, and has worked as a freelance writer for business training. He currently teaches at Greenfield Community College and at Wesleyan University. In 1991 he was awarded a grant from the Ludwig Vogelstein Foundation to continue work on a book-length poem that uses as a pretext Paul Gauguin's painting *Where Do We Come From? What Are We? Where Are We Going?*

The Contemporary Poetry Series

*Edited by Paul Zimmer*

Dannie Abse, *One-Legged on Ice*
Susan Astor, *Dame*
Gerald Barrax, *An Audience of One*
Tony Connor, *New and Selected Poems*
Franz Douskey, *Rowing Across the Dark*
Lynn Emanuel, *Hotel Fiesta*
John Engels, *Vivaldi in Early Fall*
John Engels, *Weather-Fear: New and Selected Poems*, 1958–1982
Brendan Galvin, *Atlantic Flyway*
Brendan Galvin, *Winter Oysters*
Michael Heffernan, *The Cry of Oliver Hardy*
Michael Heffernan, *To the Wreakers of Havoc*
Conrad Hilberry, *The Moon Seen as a Slice of Pineapple*
X. J. Kennedy, *Cross Ties*
Caroline Knox, *The House Party*
Gary Margolis, *The Day We Still Stand Here*
Michael Pettit, *American Light*
Bin Ramke, *White Monkeys*
J. W. Rivers, *Proud and on My Feet*
Laurie Sheck, *Amaranth*
Myra Sklarew, *The Science of Goodbyes*
Marcia Southwick, *The Night Won't Save Anyone*
Mary Swander, *Succession*
Bruce Weigl, *The Monkey Wars*
Paul Zarzyski, *The Make-Up of Ice*

# The Contemporary Poetry Series

*Edited by Bin Ramke*

J. T. Barbarese, *New Science*
J. T. Barbarese, *Under the Blue Moon*
Scott Cairns, *Figures for the Ghost*
Scott Cairns, *The Translation of Babel*
Richard Chess, *Tekiah*
Richard Cole, *The Glass Children*
Martha Collins, *A History of a Small Life on a Windy Planet*
Juan Delgado, *Green Web*
Wayne Dodd, *Echoes of the Unspoken*
Wayne Dodd, *Sometimes Music Rises*
Joseph Duemer, *Customs*
Candice Favilla, *Cups*
Casey Finch, *Harming Others*
Norman Finkelstein, *Restless Messengers*
Dennis Finnell, *Belovèd Beast*
Karen Fish, *The Cedar Canoe*
Albert Goldbarth, *Heaven and Earth: A Cosmology*
Jonathan Holden, *American Gothic*
Maurice Kilwein Guevara, *Postmortem*
Caroline Knox, *To Newfoundland*
Steve Kronen, *Empirical Evidence*
Patrick Lawler, *A Drowning Man Is Never Tall Enough*
Sydney Lea, *No Sign*
Jeanne Lebow, *The Outlaw James Copeland and the Champion-Belted Empress*
Phillis Levin, *Temples and Fields*
Gary Margolis, *Falling Awake*
Jacqueline Osherow, *Conversations with Survivors*
Jacqueline Osherow, *Looking for Angels in New York*
Donald Revell, *The Gaza of Winter*
Martha Clare Ronk, *Desire in L.A.*
Aleda Shirley, *Chinese Architecture*
Susan Stewart, *The Hive*
Terese Svoboda, *All Aberration*
Terese Svoboda, *Mere Mortals*
Arthur Vogelsang, *Twentieth Century Women*
Sidney Wade, *Empty Sleeves*
Marjorie Welish, *Casting Sequences*
Susan Wheeler, *Bag 'o' Diamonds*
C. D. Wright, *String Light*